OuR Vote is our Voice

Stories of Heroic Americans Who Fought for Our Rights

Written and Illustrated by

Hendrix, Phebe, Ellis, Colin, John, Ryan, Matea, Grace, Max, Karina, Nora, Addy, Myan, Eli, Alex, Henry, Jessara, Landon & Aida

With love and support from author Alex McConduit, illustrator Irwan Awalludin & their 3rd Grade Teacher Jake Chernikoff

This book is dedicated to everyone who came before us that fought for the voices of the voiceless. It is also dedicated to all of the children who will continue to rise up for a better world for future generations.

Shortly after we wrote this book, Congressman John Lewis passed away. As Congresswoman Terri Sewell said on the day of his memorial service, the people in this book like Congressman Lewis *"gave us the road map... All we have to do is dare to follow it"*.

Acknowledgements

The wonderful students of Room 110 would also like to thank the many people who made this project possible. Thank you to our families who read and wrote with us, asked and answered questions, and encouraged us throughout this process. Thank you to Alex McConduit who tirelessly brought his enthusiasm and expertise to the writing, editing and publishing of this book. Thank you to Irwan Awalludin who worked with our class and helped to bring the students' vision and creativity to life in the artwork that you see in this book. Thank you to Pete Carlsson who worked tirelessly to make this project a reality through its design and layout. Thank you to Jeff Furman and Rejoice the Vote for the initial challenge and inspiration for this book. Thank you to Laura Branca of the Dorothy Cotton Institute and Phoebe Brown from the Alliance of Families for Justice for the opportunity to interview them and learn about their stories and those who inspired their work. Finally, thank you to the amazing Voting Vanguards who changed history and everyone who has stood up against great odds to make a better world for us.

This book was made possible by generous grant funding from the Ithaca Public Education Initiative.

IPEI
Ithaca Public Education Initiative

Table of Contents

OUR Vote is V

Introduction

A Voting Vanguard is someone who struggled so that others could have a voice through voting. It is someone who fought against people or systems that wanted to silence the voices of others. By learning the stories shared in this book, we hope that you will carry on with the work of the brave and amazing figures who have paved the way for our freedom. At the very least, remember that by using your right to vote, you can also be a Voting Vanguard. People have fought, and even died, for our rights, so remember to never take them for granted.

our

oice

John Lewis
By Alex & Matea

EDMUND PETTUS BRIDGE

For his entire life, John Lewis has used his voice to ensure the civil rights and economic rights of all Americans. As a young man, John was inspired by major figures in the fight for civil rights and learned a lot from them. He joined the movement at a very early age and became one of the most memorable figures from this time. Lewis took everything he learned and eventually became a U.S. Congressman where he continues to fight to this day.

John Lewis led an amazing life. When he was a very young man, he worked with Dr. Martin Luther King Jr. He took part in the famous March on Washington in 1963 when he was only 23 years old. Lewis was the youngest speaker to take part in this historic occasion. Throughout his entire life, John Lewis continued to fight for what he believed was right despite the consequences. Over his decades of marching, protesting and speaking out, he went to jail 45 times and was even attacked and injured by those who wanted to silence his voice, but he fought and didn't give up.

One thing that John Lewis has always stood up and fought for is people's right to vote. Throughout his life he has marched, protested and worked to change laws so that everyone can have the right to vote. In 1965, John Lewis was one of the main leaders of the famous march in Selma, Alabama. Lewis, along with other civil rights leaders and protestors, began a march to the state capital, Montgomery, to draw attention to the **disenfranchisement** of Black voters. Their peaceful march was stopped short at the Edmund Pettus Bridge where state troopers attacked and injured innocent marchers. The event went on to be called Bloody Sunday. John Lewis and the other organizers made sure that the whole world heard about what happened at that bridge in Selma and their fight for voting rights. This led to a new law being passed giving all people in America the right to vote. This law was called the Voting Rights Act of 1965. It was a big change in voting laws after many years of African Americans fighting for their right to vote.

John Lewis grew up during a time when Black people couldn't vote, but through his work and the work of others he was able to witness the election of President Barack Obama, America's first African American president. This moment, when Lewis was able to be by the side of the first Black president, showed that his hard work had truly made a difference in the world. In fact, in 2011, John Lewis was honored by President Obama, who gave him the Presidential Medal of Freedom to commemorate a lifetime of courage from a great man who really fought for what he believed in. John Lewis was arrested, yelled at, beaten and threatened, but he didn't give up because he wanted everyone to be treated fairly. His life and achievements show us that if you work hard for a long enough time, you can do anything.

Dorothy Cotton
By Eli, Jessara, Karina, Nora & Phebe

Dorothy Cotton was the definition of a true "shero". What's a "shero" you may ask? A shero is a woman hero who is admired for her courageous qualities. Dorothy Cotton wasn't afraid to get into trouble while standing up for people's rights. She taught people how to pass unfair voting tests and helped them register to vote, even though at the time it was very difficult. She was a peaceful protestor, and believed in using her words and not her fists.

Dorothy Cotton was a civil rights activist, educator and leader. She was born in 1930 in Goldsboro, North Carolina. Her mother died when she was only three years old and she and her sisters had to be brave from a young age while being raised by their abusive father. Dorothy was a very smart woman. She went to school at Virginia State University and then Boston University. Her high school teacher helped her to get into college and Dorothy was able to earn a Master's Degree. As she continued down her path, she gained more and more confidence along the way. She died in 2018 in Ithaca, New York. Yes, that's right, Dorothy Cotton lived the last part of her life in Ithaca, New York (right where this book is being written!) and worked for Cornell University for many years.

Most of Dorothy's greatest accomplishments happened during the Civil Rights Movement. She taught thousands how to read, write and count so that they could vote. Dorothy did this because at the time there were unfair voting tests that used ridiculous questions like, "Do you know how many bubbles are in a bar of soap?", in order to stop African Americans from voting. She was a member of many organizations and was a leader in most of them. She was the only woman on Dr. Martin Luther King's executive committee and started the Citizen Education Program with him to educate and inspire others to vote. She even wrote a book called, If Your Back's Not Bent, about her life and her work with Dr. King. Dorothy Cotton felt strongly about everyone having an equal voice. She taught others about peaceful protesting in order to be heard, but most importantly she stressed that in order to be heard, you had to vote.

Dorothy also helped in the fight against **segregation.** Segregation meant that African Americans and white people weren't allowed to do the same things or go to the same places. Dorothy Cotton organized marches and protests against segregation. During one protest, the police came and beat up the people marching. Dorothy was one of the people beaten, and she developed hearing problems in her left ear because of it. She continually put her safety at risk to help others achieve the rights they deserved. Due to her efforts and the efforts of others who were a part of the **Civil Rights** Movement, African Americans were granted many of the same rights that only white Americans previously enjoyed.

Dorothy Cotton was a hard worker and spent her life working with people from all walks of life. She lent her courage to people all over the world. Dorothy worked with protestors from South Africa all the way to Israel to help them **overcome** struggles and get the rights they deserved. She overcame the obstacles that stood in the way of African Americans and women and still found time to fight for others. Dorothy Cotton always fought for what she wanted and this is what made her a true shero!!

Elizabeth Cady Stanton
By Addyson & Henry

Have you ever heard of Elizabeth Cady Stanton? She was a very brave woman who used her courage to help people get equal rights in America. Stanton brought together large groups of people and inspired men and women from all around the country. She fought for many causes including the **abolition** of slavery, but mainly focused her energy on the fight for women's rights. Keep reading to learn more about Elizabeth Cady Stanton and how she inspired people around the world.

Elizabeth Cady Stanton was a woman that stood up for women's rights and for the rights of African Americans. She was born on November 12, 1819, in Johnstown, New York. She lived with her mother, Margaret Livingston Cady and her father, Judge Daniel Cady. She was the eighth out of eleven children. When she was a kid, she attended Johnstown Academy and later went to college at Troy Female Seminary in New York. After college, she married Henry Stanton and together they had seven children.

One of Elizabeth's greatest accomplishments was helping women get the right to vote. It all started at Elizabeth's friend Lucretia Mott's house. As they were talking about women not having the same rights as men, Elizabeth got an idea. If she could vote, she could change laws! So Elizabeth decided to create a large meeting to discuss these issues. On July 19, 1848, Elizabeth organized the First Women's Rights Convention in a church in Seneca Falls, New York. About 300 people attended the **convention.** Stanton made a Declaration of Sentiments with some other important women saying that they should be given equal rights, especially the right to vote. Some men signed it, too! She continued working for women's rights for her whole life. Later, in 1869, she and Susan B. Anthony created the National Woman **Suffrage** Association to further the fight for voting rights for women. Aside from her work on women's rights, Elizabeth fought for the abolition of slavery, she was a supporter of the temperance movement and helped pass other laws that supported equality for women, like being able to own their own land. Elizabeth Cady Stanton died on October 25, 1902.

One of the best things about Elizabeth Cady Stanton was her ability to bring people together. During her life, some people felt like their voices were not heard and that they did not count. By working with others and choosing to fight, Elizabeth became an **advocate** for those who could not advocate for themselves. If she did not stand up during her life, women today still might not have the right to vote. Her work changed the world and brought all Americans closer together. She was a true American hero.

Frederick Douglass
By Colin, John & Max

Have you ever heard of Frederick Douglass? Frederick Douglass was a courageous man and he did many heroic things. He was born into slavery and one day escaped. As a free man, he spoke out against **injustices** in America. He supported the **abolition** of slavery, voting rights for all, and women's rights. He was the only Black man who attended the First Women's Suffrage Convention. He taught many enslaved people how to read, and Douglass also used his life to help those without a voice be heard. Keep reading to learn more about Frederick Douglass and all the things he accomplished during his lifetime.

Frederick Douglass was a free man, but it wasn't always that way. He grew up as a slave, but didn't allow that to stop him from leading and educating others. He was taught to read by his slave master's wife until she was forced to stop. Frederick Douglass was determined to keep learning to read by watching others, even if that got him in trouble. Douglass spent his whole life fighting for freedom and equality for people around the world. He became an influential speaker at anti-slavery meetings, he started a newspaper and attended women's rights conventions. He was such an influential person that he became an advisor to Abraham Lincoln. He helped Lincoln understand that one of the goals of the Civil War should be the freedom of slaves. Frederick Douglass wrote a book about his life as a slave. People looked up to his book and began to support his ideas; even white people! His book became popular not only in the United States, but around the entire world. Friends of Frederick became worried that the fame of his book would attract the attention of his old slave master. To escape the danger he faced in America, Frederick traveled to Europe where his supporters raised funds to buy his freedom, making him a free man.

You might think that escaping from slavery would be enough, but Frederick Douglass believed that you weren't really free unless you had the right to vote. He thought it was wrong that only white men could vote. At the time, Black people and women could not vote, but his fight for voting rights included everyone! In 1848, there was a very famous meeting in Seneca Falls, NY called the Seneca Falls Convention. It was the first women's rights convention and had over 300 attendees. Frederick Douglass was one of the only men there, and was the only free Black man in attendance. Douglass spoke in support of women being able to vote at the meeting. After the convention, he continued to be a part of the women's suffrage movement and helped with their struggle. In 1866, he joined Elizabeth Cady Stanton and Susan B. Anthony to create the American Equal Rights Association. They came together to fight for **universal suffrage,** which means that every person should have the right to vote. Even though Frederick Douglass was famous for many things, he was also a very important part of the fight for voting rights in America.

As you have learned, Frederick Douglass was a very ambitious person. He helped everyone, from enslaved people all the way to President Lincoln. His story shows us all that no matter where you start in life, you can shine if you try your best. He was a great speaker, writer and human being! During his time, he became one of the most famous people in the world! So now you know that Frederick Douglass was a great person who changed the world. You should also know that if you want to, you can help change the world too!

Gerrit Smith
By Jake Chernikoff, Alex McConduit & The Students of Room 110

Have you ever heard of Gerrit Smith? Most people haven't, but everyone should learn more about him and the great things he did. Gerrit Smith spent his life fighting for the rights of others. He also used his money and influence to support others who fought for the same things he believed in.

Gerrit Smith was born in Utica, New York, in 1797, and died in 1874. He came from a wealthy family of successful businessmen. Smith went to Hamilton College in New York and then, in addition to continuing a successful life in business, he also became involved in politics. Smith ran for President of the United States three times and although he never won, he was elected to the U.S. Congress. While in Congress, he was the only member to publicly insist on his commitment to **abolition**. Smith married his second wife, Ann Carroll Fitzhugh in 1822 and had 4 children with her. His daughter, Elizabeth Smith Miller, was a social reformer and advocate for women's rights, much like her father.

During Smith's time, his views and thinking were considered very progressive. Between 1836 and 1839 Gerrit Smith served as the president of the New York Anti-Slavery Society. Smith also acted as a "station master" in the Underground Railroad, which helped enslaved people find freedom. The estate he built in New York is the place where most freed Black people from Massachusetts and New York went to find safety. Throughout his life, Smith risked his reputation, wealth and his own life to help other people get the same rights he inherited.

Gerrit Smith also fought for all people to get the right to vote. He supported the women's suffrage movement and fought for women to be treated fairly. In 1852, he spoke at the Syracuse National Convention where he called for women to be given the right to vote. Over the years, Gerrit Smith spoke openly in support of the American Woman's Suffrage Association. Smith also had a revolutionary idea when it came to helping many Black people to be able to vote. At the time, there was a law that only allowed people who owned land to vote. This was a way for the government to technically give Black people the right to vote, but then have a condition that stopped many of them from doing so. Gerrit Smith led the way and organized other people to donate enough land to many people so that they were now allowed to vote. Smith used his own personal fortune to buy land for over 3,000 Black people so that they could have a better life and rights like voting. This was a brave and creative way to make a difference and work past sneaky laws that were designed to take away people's rights.

Gerrit Smith did a lot of great things and worked with a lot of great people. He supported the famous abolitionist John Brown, mentored Frederick Douglass, and worked with Susan B. Anthony who is well known for her work in women's rights. Many people who have wealthy and comfortable lives keep those things to themselves, but Gerrit Smith was different. He used the privileges he was given in life to make the world become a better place.

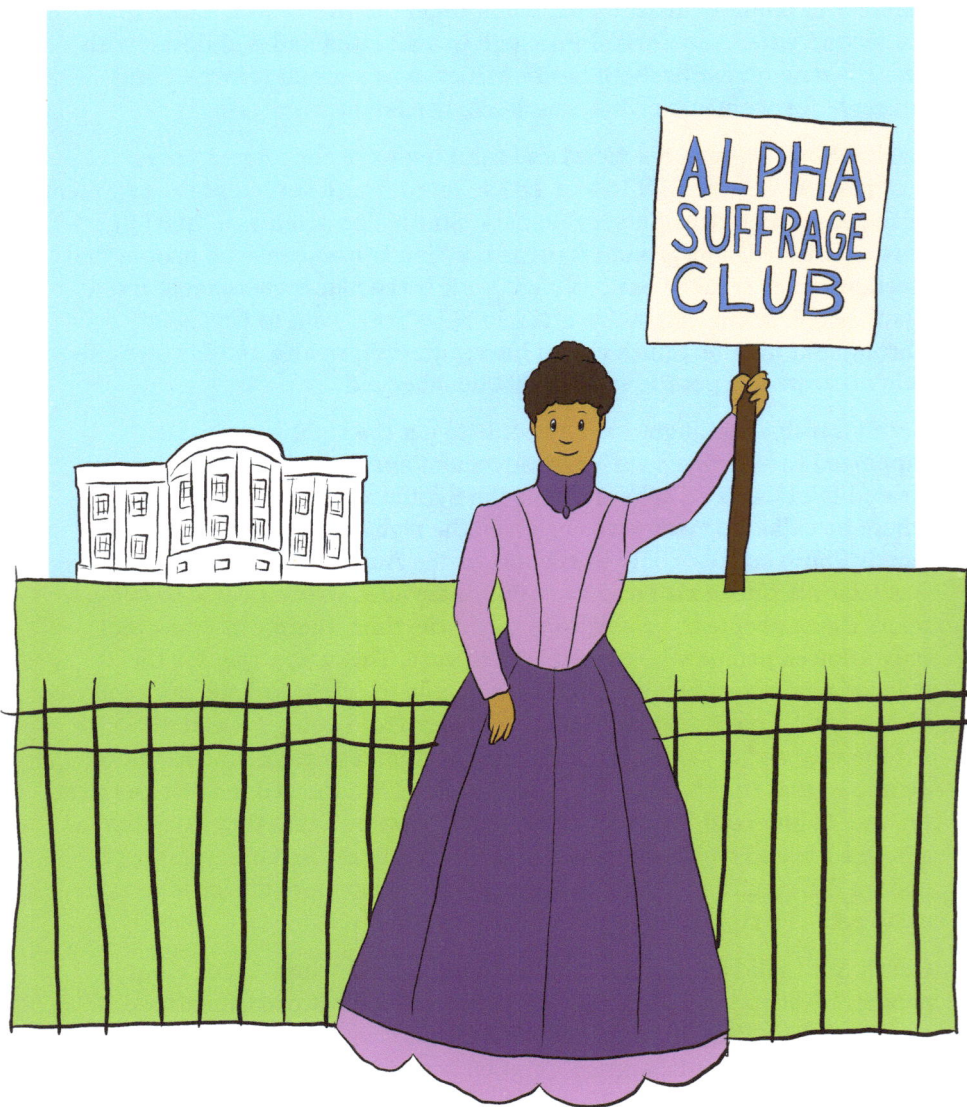

Have you ever heard of Ida B. Wells? Ida B. Wells was born into slavery in Mississippi in 1862. Her parents and her youngest brother died when she was 16 years old from Yellow Fever. Although her neighbors offered her help, Ida took care of her family by herself. Even in her childhood, you could see that Ida was a very brave person, and she brought this courage with her throughout her life. Once while riding the train, Ida was forced to ride in the back by two full grown men because she was Black. She knew that it was wrong to force people to be separated based on their race, so she took the railroad company to court and won! This showed Ida that her voice mattered and inspired her to lead a life of activism.

Ida B. Wells was an amazing person, and she helped a lot of people during her day. Even though she was born enslaved, she became a great leader. For example, in 1910 she helped W.E.B DuBois and friends create the NAACP (National Association for the Advancement of Colored People). One of their goals was to get Black people the right to vote. Ida thought everyone should have the right to vote. In 1913, she founded the Alpha Suffrage Club, and she marched in front of the White House with 5,000 women to protest for Black women to get the right to vote. Ida was also a journalist who owned and wrote her own newspaper. Her nickname was Lola of the Press and she used her pen as a way to help Black people fight for their rights. People would get angry at her but she never stopped writing about what she believed in. Clearly, Ida B. Wells made a big impact during her life.

Ida B. Wells died on March 25, 1931, at the age of 68 from kidney disease. Her brave and courageous work around voting rights helped grant women and Black people the right to vote. Ida B. Wells once said, "The people must know before they can act, and there is no educator to compare with the press." This means that people can't fix things unless they first know about them. From the time that her parents died, Ida always believed in the importance of educating and caring for others and speaking up for people who aren't always able to speak up for themselves. She lived a great life and helped so many along the way.

Jennings Randolph
By Hendrix, Myan & Ryan

VOTING RIGHTS AT 18

It takes a lot of courage to stand up for something, especially when it is unpopular with others. Throughout his life, Jennings Randolph did just that and that made him a very brave man. He believed that everyone should be able to vote while many other people thought that it was not a good rule. Jennings Randolph taught us all that if you stick to what you believe and fight for what's right, one day it just might happen.

Jennings Randolph was born March 8th, 1902, in Salem, West Virginia. Jennings was always very hard working and smart. This helped him to graduate from Salem College in only two years! His dad and grandfather were both Mayor of Salem during their lives. Although Randolph didn't become the mayor like his father and grandfather, he did end up having a life in politics. He served as a Congressman and a Senator and won six elections during his career. That's crazy!

Jennings Randolph's most famous accomplishment in politics was helping to pass the 26th Amendment, which changed the voting age from 21 to 18 years old. Randolph believed that if you could join the military at 18, you should also be able to vote for the politicians that decide if we go to war. He first introduced this bill in 1942, and it didn't pass into law until 1971. The bill to create this law was voted down 10 times, but Randolph stuck with it. On the 11th time, Congress finally passed the law, but only for national elections. Instead of being happy that the bill passed, Randolph kept fighting to get it right and finally the voting age was lowered to 18 for all elections. As a Senator he also voted for many civil rights laws that fought against things like **segregation,** and he believed that everyone should be able to vote no matter their skin color, where they lived, or what they believed in.

In addition to his political career, Jennings Randolph had different jobs throughout his life. He was a professor, worked for a newspaper and also worked for an airline. He would even sometimes fly from West Virginia to Washington D.C. multiple times in a day. Randolph loved aviation so much that he worked to create laws that would make a special museum in D.C. called the National Air and Space Museum. He even helped to start a holiday to celebrate flying every year. Randolph's diverse experiences and jobs helped him throughout his life. Due to his work and compassion, West Virginia honored Jennings Randolph by giving lakes, bridges and schools his name.

Jennings Randlolph once said, "I believe that our young people possess a great social conscience, are perplexed by the injustice which exists in the world and are anxious to rectify these ills." He always knew that it was young people that would change America for the better, and he fought for their voices to be heard, even when others did not want to hear them.

22

If you were lucky enough to have a teacher like Shirley Chisholm, you would probably never forget her. Even though she left a career in the classroom to become a politician, she never stopped teaching others. Shirley Chisolm was brave and never afraid to try new things. She was the first African American woman to run for president and although some people tried, she didn't let anyone stop her. She used her bravery to represent the voices of African Americans and all women! Shirley Chisholm once said, "You don't need to go along to get along." Throughout her life she showed that this was true by fighting for people's rights and making friends, even if she didn't always agree with them. She knew that standing up for what she believed in wouldn't always be popular, but she still did it.

Shirley Chisholm started her career in Brooklyn, NY as a teacher. Throughout the rest of her life she always showed how much she cared about kids and their families. When she became a politician, first in the New York State Assembly and then the United States Congress, she always kept them in mind. When Shirley was in Congress, more bills were sent out to benefit children, families and human rights than at any other time in the history of the U.S. Congress. So many people supported Shirley Chishlom that she was able to run for President of the United States in 1972. She was the first woman and the first African American to have a major campaign for president. Although she did not win, the issues that she cared about continued to matter because people had heard her voice.

Shirley Chisolm taught the world that even if someone isn't ready or wanting to hear what you have to say, you should still say it. Her involvement in politics was an inspiration to many. Shirley went all around the world to inspire women to think of themselves as leaders of the future. Along the way, she also inspired men to believe that women could vote and should have the same rights that they did. One of her most popular mottos was "Unbought and Unbossed!".

It doesn't matter what gender you are and it doesn't matter what color your skin is, you should always be able to be seen and heard! Shirley Chisolm used to say, "If they say there are no seats at the table, just bring a folding chair." She used this saying to inspire people to get involved in the fight for their rights.

Some people would say that Shirley Chilsolm was stubborn, but in a good way! During her life, she accomplished things that many people thought weren't possible. Her political accomplishments and her campaign to run for president paved the way for Jesse Jackson, Hillary Clinton, and Barack Obama to do the same. She inspired the entire country to think of themselves as leaders and changed America for the better.

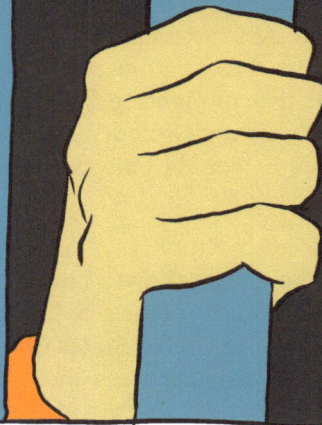

Modern Disenfranchisement

According to the Merriam-Webster dictionary, to disenfranchise is to deprive a person or a group of a legal right, *especially* the right to vote!

In America, there has been a long legacy of disenfranchisement which has shaped this country's development. During the United States' 240 year history, different groups of Americans have been disenfranchised for different reasons. You've read about the injustices that stopped some Americans from voting based on the color of their skin, their gender and even their age! You've also learned about the unfair voting requirements, intimidation tactics and illegal voting tests used in the past, but did you know that there are over 6 million people in the United States that cannot vote right now?

These 6 million-plus Americans are old enough to vote, they are citizens of the USA, and they fulfil all of the rules for being allowed to vote except for one. They've been convicted of a crime! This is called **Felony Disenfranchisement**.

In most states in the US, if you've been convicted of a crime you are at risk of losing your right to vote. If we are to believe that Our Vote is Our Voice, then this means that there are people who have their voice taken from them everyday! In 9 states some people can even lose their right to vote for the rest of their lives.

In America, all citizens are promised the right to vote. Allowing each person to vote and help create the rules they live under makes everyone more likely to follow the rules. According to the Brennan Center for Justice, *"Increased voter participation also makes our government more responsive to the diverse needs of our country."*

In our third grade class, as soon as the year began all of the students created a set of classroom expectations that everyone agreed to follow. As each student gave their opinion on the rules and watched it be written on the board, it made them all feel more invested in creating a classroom that was the way they wanted it to be. By allowing their vote to be their voice, everyone was heard and the rules that were created for the classroom reflected that! Everyone was also much more likely to follow these things since they were involved in creating them.

Unfortunately, people convicted of crimes aren't the only ones who are disenfranchised. People who live in the U.S. territory of Puerto Rico cannot vote in Presidential elections and aren't represented in Congress or the Senate, homeless people have a hard time registering to vote without stable addresses, and if you are reading this and are under the age of 18 you can't vote yet either! Fortunately, there are other ways for your voice to be heard. Here are a few ways that you can let your government representatives know what you think about modern disenfranchisement in America!

What We Can Do

- Talk to your family and friends about what matters to you.
- Encourage those who can vote to do so.
- Start a letter writing campaign, call or email government officials.
- Plan or join a protest or march.
- Attend town hall, city council, school board and other official meetings.
- Find groups and organizations who share your values and ideas. If you can't find one, start one and get the word out yourself!

The Story of this Book

On the evening of March 13th, 2020, the students and families of Ithaca, NY were told that they wouldn't be coming back to school on Monday. Covid-19 was sweeping the nation and world, and with the situation rapidly approaching a life-changing pandemic, school in the traditional sense was no longer a possibility. Everyone stayed home on Monday, and for the days, weeks and months to come. We wouldn't see each other in person again for the remainder of the year, and we went into the summer not knowing when students would return to classrooms.

Rewind to August, 2019 when a group of teachers in Ithaca met for two days in a large conference room to create "Anti-Marginalization Curriculum" for the classrooms and students of the Ithaca City School District. A specific challenge was issued by a community member named Jeff Furman: inspire kids to create excitement and change around voting. Fueled by ice cream brought by Jeff, we worked to meet and pass along his challenge and that of his newly formed initiative called Rejoice the Vote. The charge was to "honor the past, celebrate the present & challenge the future". As I began to learn about the long history of people that Rejoice the Vote called "voting vanguards", I couldn't help but envision the inspiration that my students would draw from learning about these people and their work.

There was one small problem though... The stories of these mostly unsung heroes were sometimes pretty tricky to find, especially at the level of third graders. How could I teach my students about these amazing people if there weren't really books or other resources accessible to them? That question answered itself when Alex McConduit, a visiting guest author, proposed a project. He wanted to write a book about voting, and McConduit was so impressed with our class during his visit that he thought we would be perfect candidates to help him. Lots of meetings, research, some amazing partnerships, a crucial grant (thanks, IPEI!) and some good old fashioned inspiration and perspiration later, we would research, write and publish a book.

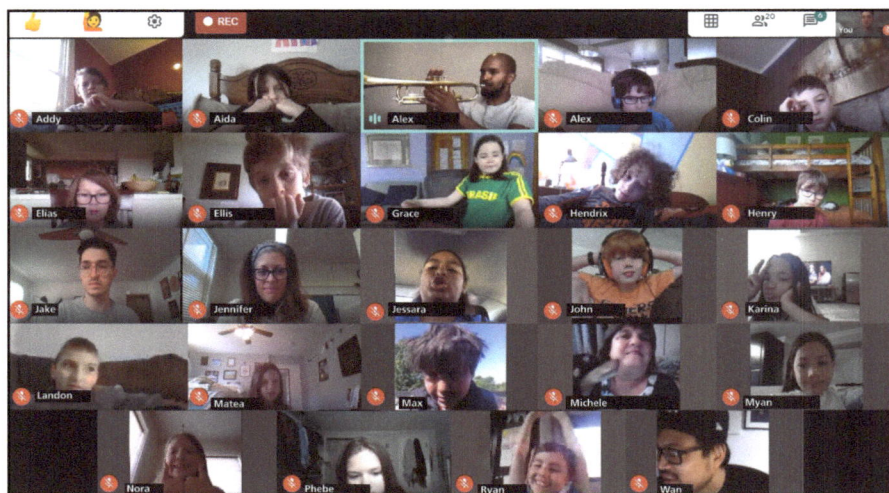

So we did it, and we did it well. Every day for a series of weeks in May and June, students signed on to meet as a class, to do their math and spelling, their keyboarding, cursive and reading, but also to create a book. They researched, interviewed, took notes, wrote, revised, edited, conferenced in teams, illustrated and fueled this project with their joy and ambition. With their faces and voices all lined up on our computer screens, they published a book. They published a great book, and an important book, and we really hope that you enjoyed it and learned something about the potential of your own voice and ambition while doing so.

- Jake Frumkin Chernikoff

Addy

Aida

Alex

Colin

Eli

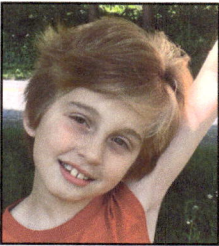
Ellis

Grace

Hendrix

Henry

Jen Ebel

Jessara

John

Karina

Landon

Matea

Max

Michelle Tagliavento

Myan

Nora

Phebe

Ryan

1

Ida B. Wells

Votes For Women

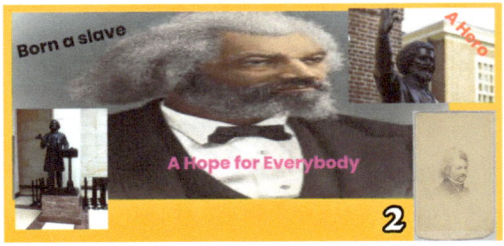

2

Born a slave

A Hero

A Hope for Everybody

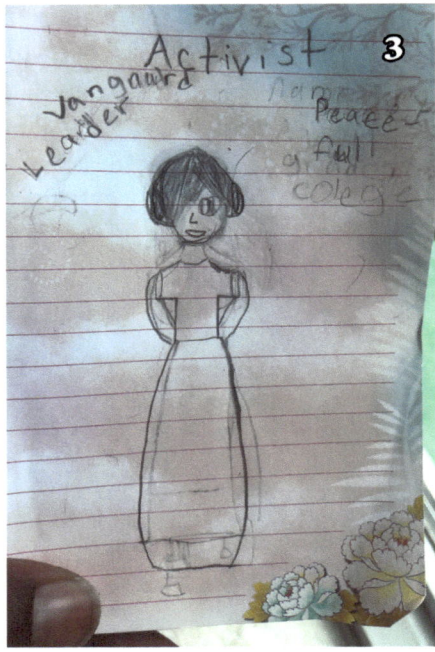

3

Activist

Vangaurd Leader

Peace full college

4

5

6

7

8

9

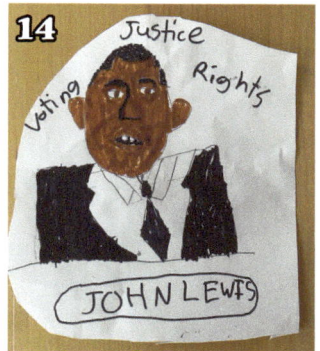

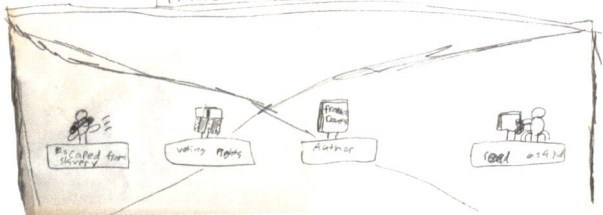

1 - **Grace** / Ida B. Wells
2 - **Max** / Frederick Douglass
3 - **Jessara** / Dorothy Cotton
4 - **Ellis** / Shirley Chisholm
5 - **Hendrix** / Jennings Randolph
6 - **Henry** / Elizabeth Cady Stanton

7 - **Alex** / John Lewis
8 - **Myan** / Jennings Randolph
9 - **Eli** / Dorothy Cotton
10 - **Colin** / Frederick Douglass
11 - **Aida** / Ida B. Wells
12 - **Nora** / Dorothy Cotton

13 - **Addy** / Elizabeth Cady Stanton
14 - **Matea** / John Lewis
15 - **John** / Frederick Douglas
16 - **Karina** / Dorothy Cotton
17 - **Phebe** / Dorothy Cotton
18 - **Ryan** / Jennings Randolph

29

Glossary

Slavery - When a person owns another person and makes them work and follow orders without pay or respect for their human rights

Voting - The process through which people express their ideas and choices to make a fair decision in a group

Disenfranchise - To take away someone's right (usually to vote)

Abolish - To stop or end a system or way of doing something. "Abolition" is often used to talk about ending slavery.

Suffrage - Having the right to vote in public political elections

Universal Suffrage - Everyone having the right to vote regardless of race, gender or any other factors

Civil Rights - Basic human rights protected by the government

Protest - The act of standing up and speaking out against what you think is wrong

Vanguard - A leader at the forefront of an idea or movement

Segregation - The act of keeping people separated. Throughout history people have been segregated based on race, gender, and who they are or what they believe.

Advocate - To speak up for or defend the rights of others

The kids did all of the hard work, but these people helped out too.

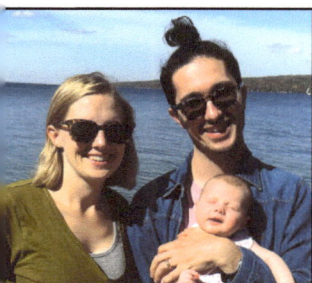

Jake Frumkin Chernikoff is a 3rd Grade teacher at South Hill Elementary School. He lives in Ithaca, NY with his wonderful wife and daughter, but will always consider New Orleans and Philadelphia home as well. His students say he is the greatest, but he's just trying to be as amazing as they are.

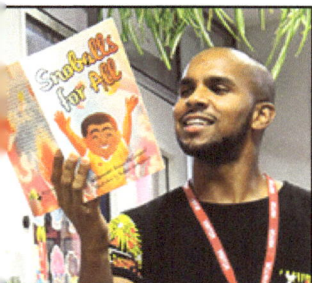

Alexander Brian McConduit is an author, educator and entrepreneur from New Orleans, LA. He used to travel the world sharing his love for his two passions, New Orleans and writing with students around the globe but now his travels are limited to his laptop!

Irwan Awalludin is a Singapore-born, Brooklyn-based, Grammy Award nominated designer. He usually works with famous rappers, but he thought that 3rd graders were pretty awesome too!

Pete Carlsson is a graphic designer and John's dad! He has been working on comics and books for over 20 years, and this is his first project with kids!

Our Vote is Our Voice is a collection of biographies written by third graders that profile some of the most important figures in the struggle for voting rights in American history. Read the stories of these true American heroes through the eyes of our young authors. Through hard work, a lot of writing and a little help from their teachers, these students have shared their work with the world in an effort to encourage everyone out there to use their voice and **VOTE!**

www.ingramcontent.com/pod-product-compliance
Lightning Source LLC
Chambersburg PA
CBHW041759040426
42447CB00001B/27

9 780985 199852